PERCEPTION MATTERS

UNLOCKING YOUR REALITY

PRASHANT ZAMBRE

Made with ♥ on the Notion Press Platform
www.notionpress.com

This book is dedicated to all those who seek to understand the power of perception and its impact on our lives. May this book serve as a guide to unlocking your reality and help you to see the world through new and enlightening perspectives. May you use the knowledge and techniques within these pages to improve your relationships, enhance your creativity, and achieve your personal and professional goals. Thank you for your dedication to personal growth and the pursuit of truth.

Contents

Foreword

In today's world, where there is so much happening around us, it is often easy to overlook the importance of perception. Perception is the lens through which we see the world and interpret our experiences. It shapes the way we interact with others, make decisions, and view ourselves. It affects our mental and physical health, our personal growth, and our success.

In "Perception Matters: Unlocking Your Reality," the author has provided an insightful and comprehensive guide to the world of perception. This book covers a range of topics, from the psychology of perception to its impact on communication, relationships, and success. It provides practical techniques for enhancing perception awareness, which can be applied in both personal and professional contexts.

The author has done an excellent job of presenting complex concepts in a clear and accessible way. They draw on real-world examples and case studies to illustrate the importance of perception and its impact on our lives. The book is not only informative but also inspiring, as it provides readers with the tools to unlock their potential and transform their lives.

I highly recommend "Perception Matters: Unlocking Your Reality" to anyone who wants to gain a deeper understanding of perception and its role in their lives. This book is an invaluable resource for anyone seeking to enhance their personal growth, communication skills, decision-making abilities, and overall well-being.

Acknowledgements

I would like to express my gratitude to all those who have contributed to the creation of this book, "Perception Matters: Unlocking Your Reality."

First and foremost, I want to thank my family for their unwavering support and encouragement throughout this journey. I could not have accomplished this without their love and understanding.

I am also deeply grateful to my friends and colleagues who have generously shared their knowledge and expertise in the field of perception. Their insights and feedback have been invaluable in shaping the ideas and concepts presented in this book.

I would like to extend a special thank you to my editor and the publishing team who have worked tirelessly to bring this book to life. Their dedication and commitment to excellence have been instrumental in making this a reality.

Finally, I want to thank the readers for their interest in this book. I hope that the insights and techniques presented in these pages will inspire you to harness the power of perception to unlock your reality and achieve your goals.

Preface

Perception is an essential part of our lives. It is how we make sense of the world around us and how we interact with others. However, many of us may not realize the impact that perception has on our daily lives. Our perception shapes how we see ourselves, others, and the world, which in turn impacts our decision making, communication, relationships, health, and even success.

"Perception Matters: Unlocking Your Reality" is a book that explores the importance of perception and how it impacts various aspects of our lives. This book is a comprehensive guide that will help you understand the various factors that influence our perception, the psychology of perception, and how perception affects our communication, personal growth, decision making, relationships, creativity, mindfulness, health, and success.

Throughout this book, we discuss various techniques for enhancing our perception awareness, including shifting our perspectives, managing cognitive biases, and utilizing mindfulness practices. The book also explores the role of social and cultural influences on our perception and how they impact our interactions with others.

In writing this book, we aim to provide readers with a valuable tool to help them unlock their true potential and transform their lives. Whether you are seeking personal growth or professional success, this book will provide you with practical strategies for enhancing your perception awareness and using it to your advantage.

We hope you find "Perception Matters: Unlocking Your Reality" informative, enlightening, and useful in your personal and professional life.

Best regards,

Prashant Zambre

I

The Power of Perception

" We don't see things as they are. We see them as we are." – Anais Nin

Welcome to "Perception Matters: Unlocking Your Reality!" In this book, we will explore the fascinating topic of perception and how it affects our lives. Perception is the way in which we interpret the world around us, and it has a powerful impact on the way we think, feel, and behave.

Introduction to the Importance of Perception

In this first chapter, we will introduce the importance of perception and the impact it has on our daily lives. Perception is a fundamental part of how we experience the world, and it influences everything from our emotions to our decision-making processes. Understanding perception and how it works is key to living a fulfilling and successful life.

Let me tell you a cute story!

A math teacher asked a six-year-old how many apples they would have if they were given one, then another, and one more.

The little boy replied confidently, "Four!" The teacher was surprised and thought the boy had misunderstood the question.

So, she asked him again, and the boy replied again, "Four!" The teacher was a bit disappointed and decided to try another approach.

She asked the boy how many strawberries he would have if he was given one, then another, and one more.

The boy looked up at her with sparkling eyes and said, "Three?" The teacher was thrilled because that was the right answer!

She then explained that the answer was the same for both apples and strawberries. But the little boy wasn't finished yet!

He said, "I have four apples!" The teacher was confused and asked him how he could have four apples.

The little boy shyly replied, "Because I already have one apple in my bag."

It just goes to show that everyone has their own unique perspective and perception of things, and that's what makes life interesting!

There are many different factors that can influence our perception, including our upbringing, our culture, our past experiences, and our current environment. In order to fully understand perception, we need to explore these different factors and how they can affect the way we interpret the world around us.

One of the most important things to understand about perception is that it is not necessarily an accurate representation of reality. Our perception can be influenced by our beliefs, biases, and expectations, which can lead us to see things in a way that is not entirely accurate. For example, if we have a belief that all dogs are dangerous, we may perceive a small, friendly dog as being threatening.

Despite this, perception is still incredibly powerful. The way we see the world around us shapes our thoughts, feelings, and behaviors, and it can have a profound impact on our lives. In this book, we will explore how to use perception as a tool for personal growth and success, and how to manage our perception to achieve our goals.

Throughout this book, we will explore different topics related to perception, including the psychology of perception, cultural and social influences on perception, perception and communication, perception and personal growth, perception and decision making, perception and relationships, perception and creativity, perception and mindfulness, perception and health, and perception and success.

Perception is the way in which we interpret the world around us, and it plays a crucial role in shaping our thoughts, feelings, and behavior. Perception is not only about how we see the world visually, but also how we interpret other sensory information, such as sound, smell, taste, and touch.

Perception is an active process that involves our brains and senses working together to create an understanding of the world around us. However, it's important to remember that our perception is not always an accurate representation of reality. Our perception can be influenced by our beliefs, biases, and expectations, which can lead us to see things in a way that is not entirely accurate.

For example, two people can witness the same event but have very different perceptions of it based on their past experiences, beliefs, and biases. This is why perception is often described as a subjective experience, as it can vary greatly from person to person.

Despite this subjectivity, perception is still incredibly powerful. The way we see the world shapes our thoughts, feelings, and behavior, and it can have a profound impact on our lives. This is why it's important to understand how perception works and how we can manage it to achieve our goals.

There are many different factors that can influence our perception, including our upbringing, our culture, our past experiences, and our current environment. Our perception can also be influenced by our emotions, attention, memory, and cognition.

For example, if we're feeling anxious, we may perceive the world around us as more threatening than it actually is.

In order to manage our perception, we need to be aware of these different factors and how they can affect the way we see the world. By understanding the impact of these factors, we can start to shift our perception in a more positive direction.

By managing our perception, we can use it as a tool for personal growth and success. By changing the way we see the world, we can change the way we think, feel, and behave. We can also improve our relationships, communication, decision-making, and creativity.

By the end of this book, you will have a better understanding of how perception works and how to use it to your advantage. You will have learned different techniques for managing your perception and for using it to improve your well-being and success. So, let's get started on this journey of exploring the fascinating and powerful world of perception!

In the following chapters of this book, we will explore different topics related to perception and how we can manage it to improve our lives. We will delve into the psychology of perception, cultural and social influences on perception, perception and communication, perception and personal growth, perception and decision making, perception and relationships, perception and creativity, perception and mindfulness, perception and health, and perception and success.

Understanding the impact of perception on our lives

The impact of perception on our lives is significant and far-reaching. Perception can influence the way we feel, think, and behave, and it can shape our experiences and relationships. Understanding the impact of perception on our lives is crucial for achieving personal growth and success.

One of the most important impacts of perception is its effect on our emotions. Our perception of a situation can determine whether we feel happy or sad, anxious or relaxed, hopeful or hopeless.

For example, if we perceive a situation as threatening, we may experience fear and anxiety, while if we perceive it as an opportunity, we may experience excitement and optimism.

Perception also plays a key role in shaping our thoughts and beliefs. Our perception of a situation can affect the way we think about it and the beliefs we hold.

For example, if we perceive a situation as challenging, we may believe that we are not capable of handling it, while if we perceive it as an opportunity, we may believe that we can overcome the challenge.

Perception can also influence our behavior. Our perception of a situation can affect the actions we take and the decisions we make.

For example, if we perceive a situation as dangerous, we may take actions to protect ourselves, while if we perceive it as safe, we may be more likely to take risks.

Our perception can also have a significant impact on our relationships with others. The way we perceive others can affect the way we interact with them, the judgments we make about them, and the way we feel about them.

For example, if we perceive someone as untrustworthy, we may be less likely to build a close relationship with them.

It's important to note that our perception is not always an accurate reflection of reality. Our perception can be influenced by our biases, beliefs, and expectations, which can lead us to see things in a way that is not entirely accurate. This is why it's important to be aware of our own perception and to take steps to manage it.

By understanding the impact of perception on our lives, we can start to take control of our perception and use it to our advantage. By shifting our perception in a more positive direction, we can improve our emotional well-being, change our beliefs, make better decisions, and improve our relationships.

In the following chapters of this book, we will explore different techniques for managing our perception and using it as a tool for personal growth and success. We will delve into the psychology of perception, cultural and social influences on perception, perception and communication, perception and personal growth, perception and decision making, perception and relationships, perception and creativity, perception and mindfulness, perception and health, and perception and success.

The impact of perception on our lives is significant and multifaceted. Perception is not only influenced by our senses and experiences but also by our expectations, beliefs, and emotions. It is a complex process that involves selecting, organizing, and interpreting sensory information to create meaning and understanding of the world around us.

One of the most important impacts of perception is on our mental and emotional well-being. Our perception of the world can either uplift or bring us down, depending on how we interpret and react to different stimuli. A negative perception of a situation can lead to stress, anxiety, and even depression, while a positive perception can promote feelings of happiness, contentment, and fulfillment. Perception, therefore, plays a significant role in shaping our emotional state and overall mental health.

Perception also affects the way we think and learn. Our perception of a situation can determine our attention and focus, and shape our beliefs and attitudes.

For example, if we perceive a situation as challenging, we may be more likely to pay attention to it and learn from it, while if we perceive it as irrelevant, we may disregard it and miss out on valuable opportunities for growth.

Furthermore, our perception shapes the way we interact with others and our relationships with them. Our perception of people and situations can affect the way we communicate, the decisions we make, and the judgments we form. For instance, if we perceive someone as hostile, we may be less likely to trust them, and this could harm our relationship. On the other hand, if we perceive someone as kind and trustworthy, we may be more open to building a deeper connection with them.

It's also important to note that perception is not always an accurate reflection of reality. Our perceptions can be influenced by a variety of factors, such as our experiences, cultural background, and personal biases. As a result, it's important to be aware of our own perceptions and to challenge them when necessary. By doing so, we can avoid making hasty judgments and decisions that may lead to negative consequences.

In conclusion, understanding the impact of perception on our lives is essential for personal growth and success. By managing our perception, we can improve our mental and emotional well-being, develop stronger relationships with others, and make better decisions. In the following chapters of this book, we will explore different factors that influence our perception and provide practical tips and techniques for managing it. So, let's continue on this journey of unlocking the power of perception and unlocking our reality!

The different factors that influence our perception

Perception is a complex process that is influenced by a wide range of factors. Some of these factors are external, such as the physical environment, while others are internal, such as our beliefs and attitudes. Understanding the different factors that influence our perception is important because it can help us to better manage our perception and make more accurate judgments about the world around us.

One of the primary external factors that influence our perception is the physical environment. Our perception is affected by the sensory information that we receive from our surroundings, such as the sights, sounds, smells, tastes, and textures. The lighting, temperature, and other physical factors of an environment can also influence our perception.

For example, a dimly lit room may create a feeling of mystery and suspense, while a brightly lit room may feel more welcoming and energizing.

Another external factor that influences our perception is social and cultural context. Our perception of a situation is often shaped by our beliefs and attitudes, which are influenced by the cultural norms and values of our society.

For example, in some cultures, it is considered rude to speak loudly in public, while in others, it is a sign of confidence and assertiveness. Similarly, our social relationships, such as our family, friends, and colleagues, can also influence our perception. We tend to perceive people we know more positively than strangers, and we may also perceive people who are similar to us more favorably than those who are different.

Internal factors also play a significant role in shaping our perception. Our expectations, beliefs, and attitudes can all influence the way we perceive the world.

For example, if we believe that people are generally trustworthy, we may be more likely to perceive others as honest and reliable. In contrast, if we have negative expectations or beliefs, we may be more likely to perceive people and situations in a negative light.

Another important internal factor that influences our perception is our emotions. Our emotional state can color our perception of a situation, making it seem more positive or negative than it actually is.

For example, if we are in a bad mood, we may perceive a situation as more stressful or challenging than if we were in a good mood.

In addition to the external and internal factors that influence our perception, there are several other important factors to consider. These factors include our attention, memory, and language.

Our attention plays a crucial role in shaping our perception. Our brains are bombarded with sensory information from our environment, and our attentional processes allow us to selectively focus on certain aspects of this information.

For example, when we're driving a car, we may focus our attention on the road ahead while filtering out the background noise from the radio. Our attention is not only affected by external stimuli but also by our internal state. Factors such as stress, fatigue, and distraction can all impact our attention and therefore our perception.

Memory also plays an important role in shaping our perception. Our past experiences and memories can influence the way we perceive new information.

For example, if we have had a negative experience with a particular type of food, we may be more likely to perceive it negatively in the future. Similarly, our memories of past events can shape our expectations and beliefs, which can in turn influence our perception of present and future situations.

Language is another factor that influences our perception. The words we use to describe a situation can influence the way we perceive it.

For example, if we describe a situation as "challenging," we may perceive it as more difficult than if we describe it as "interesting." Language can also influence our attitudes and beliefs, which can in turn shape our perception. For example, if we use language that reinforces negative stereotypes about a particular group of people, we may be more likely to perceive them in a negative light.

In conclusion, perception is a complex process that is influenced by a wide range of external and internal factors, including attention, memory, language, and more. By understanding these factors, we can better manage our perception and make more accurate judgments about the world around us. In the following chapters of this book, we will explore different techniques and strategies for managing our perception and unlocking our full potential.

II

The Psychology of Perception

In this chapter, we'll take a deep dive into the fascinating field of psychology and explore how it can help us understand the complex process of perception. Psychology is the scientific study of behavior and mental processes, including perception, cognition, and emotion.

Overview of the Psychology of Perception

Perception is a complex process that involves not only our senses but also our cognitive and emotional processes. Perception occurs when we receive sensory input from our environment, such as seeing a bird flying in the sky or smelling freshly baked cookies. Our brains then process this sensory input, and we interpret it to make sense of our world.

One of the key concepts in the psychology of perception is the idea of "bottom-up" and "top-down" processing. Bottom-up processing refers to the way our brains process sensory information from the environment, such as colors, shapes, and sounds. Top-down processing refers to the way our brains use our knowledge and expectations to interpret this sensory information.

For example, if we see a bird flying in the sky, we may use our knowledge of birds and our expectations about their behavior to interpret this sensory information.

Another important concept in the psychology of perception is the idea of perceptual constancy. Perceptual constancy refers to the way our brains perceive objects as staying the same, even when the sensory input changes.

For example, if we see a car from different angles, our brains still perceive it as the same car.

In addition to these concepts, there are several different theories and models of perception in psychology.

For example, the Gestalt psychology theory emphasizes the importance of organizing sensory information into meaningful patterns, while the ecological psychology theory emphasizes the importance of the environment in shaping perception.

Understanding the psychology of perception can help us better understand why we perceive things in certain ways, and how we can use this knowledge to improve our perception and decision-making. By becoming more aware of our cognitive biases and limitations, we can make more informed and accurate judgments about the world around us.

To elaborate more on the psychology of perception, it's important to note that our perception is not just a simple reflection of the world around us, but is rather a complex process influenced by many different factors. These factors include not only the sensory input we receive, but also our past experiences, expectations, beliefs, and emotions.

For example, let's say you see a person wearing a black hoodie and jeans walking down the street. Your perception of that person will not only be influenced by the sensory input of what you see, but also by your past experiences with people wearing similar clothing, your expectations of how people dressed in a certain way behave, and your emotions at the time.

Another important concept in the psychology of perception is attention. Attention refers to the ability to focus our awareness on specific stimuli in our environment. Our attention can be influenced by many factors, such as our goals, the salience of the stimuli, and our level of arousal.

For example, if we are searching for our keys in a cluttered room, we may use our attention to focus on specific areas or objects to help us find them.

The psychology of perception also includes the study of illusions, which are perceptual experiences that are not a true representation of reality. Illusions can be used to study how our brains process sensory information and can help us better understand the limitations and biases of our perception.

Overall, understanding the psychology of perception can help us become more aware of the different factors that influence our perception and decision-making. By recognizing and managing these factors, we can improve our ability to perceive and interpret the world around us more accurately and effectively.

The Role of Attention, Memory, and Cognition in Shaping Perception

In the previous chapter, we explored the fascinating world of the psychology of perception. We learned that perception is a complex process influenced by many different factors. In this chapter, we will focus on three of the most important factors that shape our perception: attention, memory, and cognition.

Attention is the process by which we selectively focus our awareness on certain aspects of our environment while ignoring others. Our attention is limited, and we cannot pay attention to everything around us at once. Instead, we selectively attend to things that are relevant to our goals, interests, or needs.

For example, if we are driving on the highway, we may selectively attend to the cars in front of us, while ignoring the billboards and buildings on the side of the road.

Memory is another critical factor that shapes our perception. Our past experiences and memories can influence how we perceive and interpret new information.

For example, if we have had a positive experience with a certain type of food in the past, we may be more likely to perceive that food as tasty and enjoyable in the future.

Cognition refers to the mental processes by which we acquire, process, store, and use information. Our cognition plays a significant role in shaping our perception, as it influences how we interpret and make sense of the sensory input we receive. For example, if we see a dog running towards us, our cognition may help us recognize it as a friendly pet rather than a threatening animal.

All three of these factors are closely interconnected and work together to shape our perception.

For example, our attention can influence what we remember and how we interpret new information, while our memory can influence what we attend to and how we interpret new information. Our cognition also plays a crucial role in this process, as it helps us make sense of the sensory input we receive.

let's delve a bit deeper into each of these factors and their role in shaping our perception.

Attention:

Our attention is selective, and we cannot attend to everything in our environment. Instead, we use our attention to focus on the most important and relevant information. This is a crucial aspect of perception because it helps us to filter out irrelevant information and concentrate on what matters. Attention can be influenced by various factors, including our goals, expectations, and emotions.

For example, if we are looking for our keys, our attention may be focused on the areas where we usually keep them.

Memory:

Our memory plays a vital role in shaping our perception. Our past experiences and memories can influence how we perceive and interpret new information. This is because our memories influence our expectations and our ability to recognize patterns.

For example, if we have seen a particular object before, we are more likely to recognize it when we see it again. Similarly, if we have had a negative experience with a certain type of food, we may be less likely to perceive it as enjoyable in the future.

Cognition:

Our cognition refers to the mental processes by which we acquire, process, store, and use information. Our cognition plays a significant role in shaping our perception, as it helps us to make sense of the sensory input we receive. Our cognition can be influenced by various factors, including our beliefs, values, and knowledge.

For example, if we are shown a series of letters, we may use our cognition to identify them as words or as random combinations of letters.

All of these factors work together to shape our perception, and they can interact in complex ways.

For example, our attention can influence what we remember, and what we remember can influence what we attend to in the future. Similarly, our cognition can help us make sense of what we perceive, and what we perceive can influence our beliefs and knowledge.

Understanding the role of attention, memory, and cognition in shaping our perception can help us become more aware of the limitations and biases of our perception. By recognizing and managing these biases, we can improve our ability to perceive and interpret the world around us more accurately and effectively.

The impact of beliefs and expectations on perception

Beliefs and expectations can have a significant impact on our perception. Our beliefs and expectations are shaped by our past experiences, cultural upbringing, and education, and they influence the way we perceive and interpret the world around us.

Beliefs are the ideas and assumptions we hold about the world and ourselves. They can be conscious or unconscious and can be positive or negative.

For example, if we believe that we are good at a particular task, we are more likely to perceive ourselves as successful in that task. On the other hand, if we believe that we are bad at a task, we are more likely to perceive ourselves as unsuccessful.

Expectations are our predictions about what we think will happen in a given situation. They can be based on our beliefs, past experiences, or cultural norms.

For example, if we expect to see a certain type of food in a restaurant, we are more likely to notice it when it appears on the menu. If it does not appear, we may be more likely to perceive the restaurant as not meeting our expectations.

Our beliefs and expectations can also create perceptual biases. These biases can lead us to see and interpret things in a certain way that may not be accurate.

For example, confirmation bias is the tendency to interpret information in a way that confirms our existing beliefs. If we believe that a particular politician is corrupt, we may be more likely to interpret their actions as corrupt, even if the evidence suggests otherwise.

Cultural factors can also play a role in shaping our beliefs and expectations. Our cultural upbringing can influence our perception of various aspects of the world, including gender roles, social norms, and religious beliefs.

For example, in some cultures, eye contact is seen as a sign of respect and honesty, while in others, it may be seen as a sign of aggression.

The impact of beliefs and expectations on perception highlights the importance of self-awareness and critical thinking. By recognizing and examining our beliefs and expectations, we can better understand how they may be influencing our perception and decision-making. We can also challenge our biases and work to develop more accurate and objective ways of perceiving the world around us.

Beliefs and expectations play a significant role in shaping our perception of the world around us. Our beliefs and expectations can lead us to selectively attend to and interpret information in ways that support our existing beliefs, even if the evidence suggests otherwise. This can create perceptual biases that can influence our decision-making and behavior.

One common perceptual bias is confirmation bias, which is the tendency to interpret information in a way that confirms our existing beliefs.

For example, if we believe that a particular political party is bad, we may be more likely to interpret their actions as negative, even if the evidence suggests otherwise. This bias can lead to polarization and prejudice in our beliefs and perceptions.

Cultural factors can also influence our beliefs and expectations, and consequently our perception. Our cultural upbringing shapes our perception of various aspects of the world, including social norms, gender roles, and religious beliefs.

For example, in some cultures, individualism is valued, and people are encouraged to express themselves and their opinions openly. In other cultures, collectivism is valued, and people are encouraged to prioritize the group's goals over their individual goals.

Our beliefs and expectations can also influence our perception of ourselves. If we believe that we are capable and competent, we are more likely to perceive ourselves as successful in various situations. On the other hand, if we have low self-esteem and doubt our abilities, we are more likely to perceive ourselves as unsuccessful.

Cognitive processes, such as attention and memory, can also be influenced by our beliefs and expectations. If we have a preconceived notion of what to expect in a particular situation, we may selectively attend to and remember information that confirms our expectations while ignoring information that contradicts them.

In summary, our beliefs and expectations have a powerful impact on our perception. By recognizing and examining our beliefs and expectations, we can become more aware of how they influence our perception and decision-making. This can help us develop more accurate and objective ways of perceiving the world around us, and can help us to avoid the negative effects of perceptual biases.

III

Perception and Communication

Perception and communication are closely related. Our perception of other people and their communication shapes our understanding of the world around us. In this chapter, we will explore the relationship between perception and communication, the ways in which differences in perception can lead to miscommunication, and techniques for improving communication through perception awareness.

Perception and communication are two interrelated processes that play a significant role in our daily lives. Perception is the process by which we select, organize, and interpret information received through our senses. It is influenced by various factors such as our past experiences, expectations, emotions, and cultural background. Communication, on the other hand, is the exchange of information, ideas, and thoughts between two or more individuals through verbal and nonverbal means.

Perception plays a crucial role in communication because our perceptions can affect the way we interpret and respond to messages from others. For instance, if we perceive someone as being rude, we may be more likely to interpret their words or actions as negative, even if they are not intended that way. Similarly, our perceptions of ourselves, including our self-concept and self-esteem, can influence how we communicate with others.

Miscommunication can occur when there are differences in perception between the sender and receiver of a message. These differences may be due to a variety of factors, including cultural differences, language barriers, emotional states, and cognitive biases.

For example, a person from a culture that values direct communication may find it difficult to understand someone from a culture that values indirect communication.

To improve communication and reduce the chances of miscommunication, it is important to be aware of our own perceptions and biases, as well as those of others. Active listening, asking clarifying questions, and paying attention to nonverbal cues can help us better understand the intended message. It is also important to be aware of cultural differences and to avoid making assumptions about someone's beliefs or values based on their background.

In conclusion, perception and communication are closely intertwined processes that impact our daily lives. Awareness of our own perceptions and biases, as well as those of others, can help us communicate more effectively and reduce the chances of miscommunication.

Exploring the relationship between perception and communication

The relationship between perception and communication is a complex and dynamic one, with each influencing the other in multiple ways. Perception influences the way we interpret and respond to communication, and communication can also shape our perceptions.

Perception can affect communication in several ways.

For example, a person's perception of their own abilities or the abilities of others can impact how they communicate. If someone believes they are not good at public speaking, they may be more hesitant to speak up in a group setting. Similarly, if someone perceives someone else as not being competent, they may be more dismissive of their ideas or input.

On the other hand, communication can also shape our perceptions. The way a message is communicated can influence how we interpret it.

For example, the tone of voice or nonverbal cues like facial expressions can convey emotion and influence how the message is received. Additionally, the context in which a message is delivered can also influence perception. For instance, a message delivered in a positive, supportive environment may be perceived more favorably than the same message delivered in a negative or hostile environment.

By exploring the relationship between perception and communication, we can gain a better understanding of how each affects the other. This awareness can help us be more mindful in our communication and develop strategies for more effective communication. It can also help us recognize when our perceptions may be clouding our judgment or causing misunderstandings, allowing us to approach situations with greater objectivity and clarity.

How differences in perception can lead to miscommunication

Differences in perception can lead to miscommunication. When we have different perceptions of a situation, we may interpret communication differently, leading to misunderstandings and conflict.

For example, if one person perceives a comment as a harmless joke, but another person perceives it as offensive, this can lead to tension and conflict.

Cultural differences can also influence perception and communication. Different cultures have different communication styles, and what may be considered appropriate in one culture may be perceived as inappropriate in another.

For example, in some cultures, direct communication is valued, while in others, indirect communication is preferred.

Techniques for improving communication through perception awareness

To improve communication, it is important to be aware of our own perceptions and to consider the perceptions of others. By recognizing and examining our own perceptions, we can become more aware of how they influence our communication. This can help us to avoid making assumptions and to communicate more effectively.

Active listening is an important technique for improving communication through perception awareness. By listening actively and asking clarifying questions, we can gain a better understanding of the other person's perspective and avoid miscommunication. Nonverbal communication is also important to consider, as it can provide clues about a person's perception and feelings.

Improving communication through perception awareness involves becoming more aware of our own perceptions and biases, as well as those of others, and developing strategies to communicate more effectively. Here are some techniques that can help improve communication through perception awareness:

Active listening:

Active listening involves paying attention to what the speaker is saying and seeking to understand their perspective. It involves not just hearing the words, but also paying attention to nonverbal cues like facial expressions and tone of voice. By actively listening, we can gain a deeper understanding of the message being communicated and respond in a more appropriate way.

Clarifying questions:

Asking clarifying questions can help to ensure that we have understood the message correctly. When we are unsure about the meaning of a message, we can ask the speaker to clarify their intent or provide more information. This can help to reduce misunderstandings and ensure that the message is received as intended.

Avoiding assumptions:

Assumptions are beliefs or judgments that we make about a situation or person without having all the facts. Avoiding assumptions means being aware of our own biases and prejudices and seeking to understand the other person's perspective before making a judgment. This can help to reduce misunderstandings and promote more effective communication.

Empathy:

Empathy involves putting ourselves in the other person's shoes and trying to understand their perspective. It involves recognizing their emotions and responding with sensitivity and understanding. By showing empathy, we can build stronger relationships and promote more effective communication.

Mindfulness:

Mindfulness involves being present in the moment and fully engaged in the communication process. It involves focusing our attention on the speaker and being aware of our own thoughts and emotions. By being more mindful, we can improve our communication skills and reduce the chances of miscommunication.

By practicing these techniques, we can improve our communication skills and promote more effective communication. By being more aware of our own perceptions and biases, as well as those of others, we can build stronger relationships, reduce misunderstandings, and create a more positive and productive communication environment.

IV

Perception and Personal Growth

Perception is a powerful tool that can be used to facilitate personal growth and transformation. Our perceptions are shaped by our past experiences, beliefs, and attitudes, which in turn shape our thoughts, emotions, and behaviors. By changing our perceptions, we can change the way we think and feel about ourselves and the world around us, and ultimately transform our lives.

One way that perception can facilitate personal growth is by enabling us to see opportunities in challenges. When we face difficult situations or obstacles, our perceptions can either limit us or inspire us to find new solutions. By shifting our perception, we can open ourselves up to new possibilities and overcome challenges more effectively.

Perception can also be used to improve our relationships with others. By becoming more aware of our own perceptions and biases, we can better understand the perspectives of others and communicate more effectively. This can lead to greater empathy and understanding, which in turn can lead to deeper and more meaningful relationships.

Another way that perception can facilitate personal growth is by helping us to identify our strengths and weaknesses. By examining our own perceptions of ourselves, we can gain insight into our own abilities and limitations, and use this knowledge to set goals and make positive changes in our lives.

Finally, perception can facilitate personal growth by helping us to cultivate a more positive and optimistic outlook on life. By focusing on the positive aspects of our lives and embracing a growth mindset, we can create a more fulfilling and meaningful life.

Overall, perception is a powerful tool that can be used to facilitate personal growth and transformation. By becoming more aware of our own perceptions and biases, we can learn to see the world in a more positive and productive light, and ultimately transform our lives in meaningful ways.

How our perception can be a tool for personal growth and transformation

Our perception is not only a way of interpreting the world around us, but it can also be a tool for personal growth and transformation. When we become more aware of our own perceptions and biases, we can use this knowledge to understand ourselves better, develop our strengths, and work on our weaknesses.

Our perceptions are shaped by our past experiences, beliefs, and attitudes, and they can either limit us or inspire us to achieve our goals. For instance, if we perceive a situation as a failure, we might feel discouraged and give up. But if we perceive it as an opportunity to learn and grow, we might feel more motivated to try again and work harder.

By becoming more aware of our perceptions, we can also learn to control them and shape them to better serve us. We can challenge our negative thoughts and beliefs, and replace them with more positive and empowering ones. This can help us overcome fears, build self-confidence, and achieve our goals.

Perception can also be a powerful tool for personal transformation. By changing the way we see ourselves and the world, we can transform our lives in meaningful ways. For instance, if we perceive ourselves as victims of circumstance, we might feel powerless to change our lives. But if we perceive ourselves as agents of change, we can take control of our lives and make positive changes.

Overall, our perception can be a valuable tool for personal growth and transformation. By becoming more aware of our perceptions and biases, we can learn to control and shape them to better serve us, overcome our limitations, and achieve our goals. It is up to us to use our perceptions as a tool for personal growth and transformation, and create the life we want to live.

Techniques for shifting perception to improve well-being and personal success

There are several techniques that can help us shift our perception to improve our well-being and personal success. Here are a few examples:

Mindfulness:

Mindfulness is the practice of being fully present and aware of our thoughts, feelings, and physical sensations. By becoming more aware of our perceptions and how they impact our experiences, we can start to shift them in a more positive direction.

Mindfulness practices like meditation and breathing exercises can help us develop greater self-awareness and control over our thoughts and emotions.

Reframing:

Reframing is the process of looking at a situation from a different perspective. By reframing a negative experience or thought, we can shift our perception to see the positive aspects of it.

For example, if we fail at something, we can reframe it as a learning opportunity rather than a personal failure. This can help us feel more optimistic and motivated to try again.

Positive self-talk:

Our internal dialogue can greatly impact our perception of ourselves and the world. By using positive self-talk, we can shift our perception to a more positive and empowering one.

For example, instead of saying "I'm not good enough", we can say "I'm capable of learning and growing". This can help us build self-confidence and a more positive outlook on life.

Gratitude:

Gratitude is the practice of focusing on the positive aspects of our lives and being thankful for them. By focusing on what we have rather than what we lack, we can shift our perception to a more positive one. Gratitude practices like keeping a gratitude journal or expressing gratitude to others can help us cultivate a more positive outlook on life.

Visualization:

Visualization is the practice of creating mental images of our desired outcomes. By visualizing ourselves succeeding and achieving our goals, we can shift our perception to a more positive and empowered one. Visualization practices like creating a vision board or guided visualization exercises can help us develop a clearer vision of what we want to achieve and how to get there.

By practicing these techniques and others, we can shift our perception to improve our well-being and personal success. While it may take time and effort to change our perceptions, the benefits of a more positive and empowering outlook on life can be well worth it.

V

Perception and Decision Making

Perception plays a vital role in our decision-making process. Our perceptions shape our understanding of the world, and this understanding is the basis of the choices we make. This chapter will explore the relationship between perception and decision making, and how our perceptions can influence the decisions we make.

The Impact of Perception on Decision Making:

Our perceptions can significantly impact our decision-making process. Our beliefs, values, biases, and expectations all shape our perceptions of a situation, which, in turn, influences our decision making. For instance, if we perceive a situation as threatening, we may make a more cautious decision than if we perceive it as safe. Similarly, if we perceive a person as untrustworthy, we may be less likely to do business with them.

Differences in Perception and Decision Making:

Individuals can have vastly different perceptions of the same situation. This can lead to differences in decision-making. For instance, two people can interpret the same data differently and make different decisions based on that interpretation. Understanding these differences in perception can help us work more effectively in groups, communicate more clearly, and make better decisions.

Techniques for improving Perception and Decision Making:

There are techniques that we can use to improve our perception and decision-making skills. One such technique is to analyze our thought patterns and challenge any biases we may hold. We can also gather more information and perspectives to make more informed decisions. Additionally, we can seek feedback from others to gain insights into our perception and decision-making processes.

Another technique is to create a decision-making framework that takes our perceptions into account. For example, we can identify our values, beliefs, and biases and use them to make more consistent and aligned decisions. By developing a framework that considers our perceptions, we can make more informed decisions that align with our goals and values.

Perception and decision making are deeply intertwined. Our perceptions can shape our understanding of a situation, influencing the choices we make. By understanding the impact of perception on decision making and using techniques to improve our perception and decision-making skills, we can make more informed and effective decisions. The more we understand our perceptions and how they shape our decisions, the better we can navigate complex situations and make choices that align with our goals and values.

The role of perception in decision making and problem solving

Perception is critical to decision-making and problem-solving, and it can impact the outcomes of these processes. Our perception influences how we interpret information, and this interpretation drives the decisions and actions we take.

When making decisions or solving problems, our perceptions influence the way we approach the situation. Our biases, experiences, and beliefs can shape how we perceive a problem and can even impact our ability to identify the root cause of an issue. For example, if we perceive a problem as being caused by someone else, we may not be able to see the role we played in the issue.

To improve decision-making and problem-solving, it is essential to understand how our perceptions influence these processes. By becoming aware of our biases, we can work to eliminate them or mitigate their impact. For example, we can take steps to gather multiple perspectives or engage in critical thinking to challenge our assumptions and biases.

Additionally, it's essential to recognize that our perceptions can impact the way we frame a problem. By framing a problem differently, we can approach it from a new perspective and develop new solutions. For example, if we frame a problem as an opportunity rather than a roadblock, we may be more inclined to explore creative solutions.

In conclusion, our perception plays a critical role in decision-making and problem-solving. By becoming aware of our biases, challenging our assumptions, and framing problems differently, we can make more informed and effective decisions and develop more innovative solutions to complex problems.

The impact of cognitive biases and heuristics on perception and decision making

Cognitive biases and heuristics can significantly impact our perception and decision-making processes. Biases are mental shortcuts that our brains take to process information, while heuristics are general problem-solving strategies that we use to make quick decisions. While these can be useful in some situations, they can also lead to errors in perception and decision-making.

For example, confirmation bias is a cognitive bias that occurs when we seek out information that confirms our existing beliefs and ignore information that contradicts them. This can lead to flawed decisions and prevent us from considering alternative viewpoints. Similarly, the availability heuristic occurs when we overestimate the importance of information that is readily available, which can also lead to poor decisions.

To mitigate the impact of cognitive biases and heuristics, it's essential to become aware of them and actively work to challenge them. For example, we can seek out information that contradicts our beliefs or use decision-making frameworks that incorporate multiple perspectives. Additionally, slowing down our decision-making process and engaging in critical thinking can also help us identify and address biases and heuristics.

Ultimately, the impact of cognitive biases and heuristics on perception and decision-making highlights the importance of being aware of our mental processes and actively working to improve them. By doing so, we can make more informed and effective decisions, even in the face of uncertainty and complexity.

Strategies for making better decisions through perception management

Perception management refers to the process of consciously controlling and shaping our perception to achieve a specific outcome. This can be a useful strategy for improving our decision-making processes, as it allows us to approach a problem or situation from a more deliberate and objective perspective. Here are some strategies for making better decisions through perception management:

Identify your biases:

As we discussed earlier, biases can significantly impact our perception and decision-making processes. The first step to managing perception is to identify our own biases and recognize when they might be influencing our decisions.

Consider multiple perspectives:

To make a well-informed decision, it's important to consider multiple perspectives and weigh the pros and cons of each option. By considering alternative viewpoints, we can gain a more comprehensive understanding of a problem and make a more informed decision.

Gather relevant information:

To make an informed decision, it's important to gather relevant information from credible sources. This can include conducting research, consulting with experts, and seeking out different opinions.

Engage in critical thinking:

Critical thinking involves questioning assumptions, evaluating evidence, and considering multiple perspectives. By engaging in critical thinking, we can identify potential biases and evaluate information more objectively.

Manage your emotions:

Our emotions can also influence our perception and decision-making processes. To make better decisions, it's important to manage our emotions and approach the situation with a clear and level head.

By using these strategies, we can improve our decision-making processes and make more informed and effective decisions. While it can be challenging to manage our perception and biases, being aware of them and actively working to challenge them can ultimately lead to better outcomes.

VI

Cultural and Social Influences on Perception

Our perception is shaped not only by our individual experiences and biases, but also by the cultural and social context in which we live. Cultural and social influences can significantly impact the way we perceive the world around us, and understanding these influences is crucial for developing a more comprehensive understanding of perception.

Cultural Influences on Perception:

Culture refers to the shared values, beliefs, and practices of a group of people. Cultural influences can impact perception in several ways, including:

Language:

The language we speak can shape the way we perceive and understand the world. For example, different languages may have different words for colors or emotions, which can impact the way we perceive and interpret these concepts.

Social norms:

Social norms refer to the unwritten rules that guide behavior within a culture. These norms can impact the way we perceive certain behaviors or actions. For example, in some cultures, it may be considered rude to make direct eye contact, while in others it may be a sign of respect.

Beliefs and values:

Our beliefs and values are shaped by the cultural context in which we live, and can significantly impact the way we perceive and interpret information. For example, individuals from collectivist cultures may prioritize group harmony over individual success, which can impact the way they perceive and respond to social situations.

Social Influences on Perception:

Social influences refer to the impact that other people have on our perceptions and behaviors. Social influences can impact perception in several ways, including:

Social roles:

Our social roles, such as our gender, race, or occupation, can impact the way we perceive and interpret information. For example, a woman may be perceived as more emotional than a man, due to gender stereotypes.

Group membership:

The groups we belong to can significantly impact the way we perceive and interpret information. This can include our racial, ethnic, or religious group, as well as our social or professional networks.

Social influence:

The behavior of others can impact our perception and decision-making processes. This can include peer pressure, conformity, or the influence of authority figures.

Understanding these cultural and social influences is crucial for developing a more comprehensive understanding of perception, and for improving our ability to interact with people from different backgrounds.

Here are some strategies for managing cultural and social influences on perception:

Be aware of your own biases:

Understanding your own cultural and social background, and how it influences your perception, is crucial for interacting with people from different backgrounds.

Engage in cross-cultural communication:

By actively seeking to understand and engage with people from different cultural and social backgrounds, we can develop a more comprehensive understanding of perception.

Avoid stereotypes:

Stereotypes can significantly impact our perception of others. By avoiding stereotypes and focusing on individual characteristics and experiences, we can develop more meaningful and productive relationships with people from different backgrounds.

Engage in critical thinking:

By engaging in critical thinking and questioning assumptions, we can identify potential biases and evaluate information more objectively.

By understanding these cultural and social influences on perception, and developing strategies for managing them, we can improve our ability to interact with people from different backgrounds and develop a more comprehensive understanding of perception.

The impact of culture and social norms on perception

Culture and social norms play a significant role in shaping our perceptions. The values, beliefs, and practices of our culture and the social groups to which we belong can influence how we perceive the world around us.

For example, in some cultures, expressing emotion is highly valued and considered a sign of strength, while in others, emotional expression may be viewed as a weakness or lack of self-control. This can impact how individuals within these cultures perceive and interpret emotional displays.

Additionally, social norms and expectations can influence our perceptions of others.

For example, individuals who belong to a certain social group may have preconceived notions about individuals outside of their group, which can impact their perception and treatment of those individuals. This is known as in-group bias, which can lead to stereotypes, prejudice, and discrimination.

Cultural and social influences on perception can also impact the way we interpret nonverbal communication, such as body language and facial expressions.

For example, a gesture that is considered rude or disrespectful in one culture may be perfectly acceptable in another.

It is important to recognize and understand the impact of culture and social norms on perception, as this can help us to avoid misunderstandings and promote greater intercultural understanding and respect. By being aware of our own cultural biases and perspectives, and by actively seeking to understand the perspectives of others, we can improve our ability to communicate and connect with people from diverse backgrounds.

Now, we will discuss how cultural and social influences on perception can impact intercultural communication.

Intercultural communication refers to communication between individuals from different cultural backgrounds. Because culture and social norms influence perception, intercultural communication can be challenging. Cultural differences can lead to misunderstandings, misinterpretations, and conflicts. In this section, we will explore how cultural and social influences on perception impact intercultural communication and discuss strategies for improving intercultural communication.

One major challenge of intercultural communication is the potential for cultural misunderstandings. This can occur when individuals from different cultures interpret the same situation or message in different ways.

For example, a gesture or facial expression that is common and understood in one culture may be misinterpreted or misunderstood by someone from a different culture.

Another challenge of intercultural communication is the potential for stereotypes and prejudice. Preconceived notions about individuals from different cultures can lead to biased perceptions and negative attitudes. Stereotypes and prejudice can be harmful and can hinder effective communication and collaboration.

To overcome these challenges, it is important to develop intercultural communication skills. This includes being aware of our own cultural biases and perspectives, as well as actively seeking to understand the perspectives of others.

Some strategies for improving intercultural communication include:

Developing cultural awareness and understanding:

By learning about different cultures and their values, beliefs, and practices, we can better understand and appreciate the perspectives of others.

Practicing active listening:

Active listening involves paying attention to the speaker and trying to understand their perspective. This can help to avoid misunderstandings and misinterpretations.

Avoiding stereotypes and prejudice:

By recognizing and challenging our own biases and prejudices, we can avoid negative attitudes and perceptions of individuals from different cultures.

Being flexible and adaptable:

Being open-minded and adaptable can help us to navigate cultural differences and communicate effectively with individuals from different cultures.

In summary, cultural and social influences on perception can impact intercultural communication. By developing intercultural communication skills and strategies, we can overcome these challenges and promote greater understanding and collaboration across cultures.

How socialization and upbringing shape perception

Our socialization and upbringing play a crucial role in shaping our perception of the world. From an early age, we are exposed to cultural and social norms that influence the way we perceive and interpret our experiences. These norms can include things like gender roles, cultural traditions, and religious beliefs.

For example, in some cultures, eye contact is a sign of respect and attentiveness, while in others, it is considered rude or confrontational. Similarly, different cultures may place varying degrees of importance on family, community, and individualism. These cultural norms and values can shape our beliefs and expectations, which in turn can impact the way we perceive and respond to different situations.

Our upbringing can also have a significant impact on our perception. Our early experiences and interactions with family, friends, and authority figures can shape our attitudes and beliefs about the world. For instance, children who grow up in households where creativity and exploration are encouraged may develop a more open and curious mindset, while those who are raised in more restrictive or authoritarian environments may be more inclined to follow rules and conform to societal norms.

It is also important to note that socialization and upbringing can create biases and prejudices that can affect how we perceive and interact with others. For example, someone who grows up in a community with a history of racial or ethnic tension may develop biases towards certain groups, which can affect their perception and behavior towards those individuals.

Understanding how socialization and upbringing impact our perception is important for developing empathy and understanding towards those with different backgrounds and experiences. It can also help us recognize and challenge our own biases, leading to a more open and inclusive mindset.

The influence of media and advertising on perception

The media, including advertising, plays a significant role in shaping our perceptions of the world around us. The constant bombardment of messages from TV, print, and online media can shape our opinions, beliefs, and attitudes towards a variety of topics, from products to politics.

Media and advertising often use tactics such as emotional appeals, social proof, and authority figures to influence our perceptions. Emotional appeals aim to create an emotional connection between the audience and the product, often by using images or stories that evoke a specific emotion. Social proof is the idea that people are more likely to believe and act on information if they believe that others also believe and act on it. Authority figures, such as celebrities or experts, are often used to endorse products or ideas, which can further influence our perception.

The influence of media and advertising on our perception is especially relevant in today's digital age, where we are constantly connected to social media platforms and online content. Online advertising can target individuals based on their browsing history and interests, tailoring the advertising message to their unique preferences and biases.

It's essential to be aware of the influence of media and advertising on our perception and to critically evaluate the messages we are exposed to. By doing so, we can make more informed decisions and develop a more accurate and nuanced understanding of the world around us.

The media and advertising are two powerful forces that shape our perceptions of the world around us. These industries use a wide range of techniques to influence our thoughts, beliefs, and values, which in turn can affect how we perceive the world.

One way that media and advertising can influence our perception is through the use of images and language. Advertisements and media outlets often use carefully selected images and language to create a specific impression or emotional response. For example, an advertisement for a luxury car might use sleek images and language that conveys a sense of power and prestige, which can influence our perceptions of the brand and the people who drive those cars.

Another way that media and advertising can influence perception is through the use of repetition. When we are exposed to the same messages repeatedly, it can begin to shape our perception of reality. For example, if we are repeatedly exposed to images of thin, conventionally attractive people in advertisements, it can begin to shape our perception of what is considered attractive or desirable.

Media and advertising can also shape our perceptions of social issues and cultural values. The way that social issues are portrayed in the media can influence our beliefs and attitudes about those issues. For example, the way that the media portrays people from different races or ethnicities can influence our perceptions of those groups.

In addition, media and advertising can reinforce or challenge cultural norms and values. For example, advertisements that challenge traditional gender roles can influence our perceptions of what is considered acceptable behavior for men and women.

It is important to be aware of the ways that media and advertising can influence our perceptions. By critically analyzing the messages that we are exposed to, we can develop a more nuanced and informed perspective on the world around us.

VII

Perception and Relationships

Our perceptions shape the way we see the world around us and the people in it. This includes how we view and interact with the people we are in relationships with, whether they are romantic partners, friends, or family members. In this chapter, we will explore how perception impacts our relationships and how we can use perception to build stronger, more positive connections with the people in our lives.

Perception and Relationships:

Perception plays a crucial role in how we form and maintain relationships. Our initial perception of someone can heavily influence whether we choose to pursue a relationship with them or not. Once in a relationship, our perceptions of our partner can influence how we communicate, how we interpret their actions, and how we feel about the relationship overall.

One way perception can impact relationships is through the halo effect, which is the tendency to perceive someone as more attractive, intelligent, and trustworthy based on one positive trait. For example, if we perceive someone as physically attractive, we may also assume that they are kind, intelligent, and successful. This can cause us to overlook negative traits or behaviors, which can be harmful to the relationship.

Perception can also impact how we communicate with our partner. If we perceive our partner as closed off or uninterested in our conversation, we may become defensive or feel hurt, even if that was not their intention. Similarly, if we perceive our partner as critical or judgemental, we may become defensive and closed off ourselves, leading to a breakdown in communication.

How to Improve Perception in Relationships:

To improve our perceptions in relationships, it is important to become aware of our own biases and assumptions. We can do this by practicing mindfulness and self-reflection, as well as actively seeking out diverse perspectives and experiences.

We can also work to improve communication by practicing active listening, which involves fully focusing on the speaker and validating their emotions and experiences. Additionally, using "I" statements instead of "you" statements can help prevent blame and defensiveness.

It is also important to practice empathy, which involves trying to understand the other person's perspective and experiences. This can be done through open-ended questions, active listening, and validating their emotions.

Perception is a powerful force in our relationships. By becoming aware of our own biases and assumptions, practicing active listening and empathy, and seeking out diverse perspectives, we can improve our perceptions and build stronger, more positive connections with the people in our lives.

The impact of perception on relationships

Perception plays a crucial role in shaping our relationships with others. It influences the way we see, interpret, and respond to the actions and behaviors of those around us. Our perceptions can either facilitate or hinder our ability to form strong, healthy, and meaningful relationships with others.

One of the ways perception affects relationships is through the lenses we use to view others. We each have our own unique perspectives that are shaped by our past experiences, values, and beliefs. These lenses can either enhance or distort the way we see others. For example, if we have a negative perception of someone, we may be more likely to view their actions in a negative light, even if they have positive intentions.

Perception also influences our ability to empathize with others. Empathy is the ability to understand and share the feelings of others. Our ability to empathize is greatly influenced by our perceptions of others. If we view others in a positive light, we are more likely to feel empathy and understanding towards them. However, if we have negative perceptions of someone, we may find it difficult to empathize with them and understand their perspective.

Another way perception affects relationships is through our communication with others. The way we interpret and respond to the actions and behaviors of others is greatly influenced by our perceptions. For example, if we have a negative perception of someone, we may be more likely to interpret their words or actions in a negative way, even if they have positive intentions. This can lead to misunderstandings and conflicts in relationships.

Overall, the impact of perception on relationships cannot be overstated. It can either foster or hinder the growth of healthy and meaningful relationships with others. Understanding the role perception plays in our relationships can help us to become more aware of our biases and better equipped to cultivate positive connections with those around us.

How our perception of others affects our behavior towards them

Our perception of others can have a significant impact on our behavior towards them. When we perceive someone positively, we tend to be more open and friendly towards them. On the other hand, if we have a negative perception of someone, we may be more closed off or even hostile towards them.

For example, if we perceive someone as being unfriendly, we may not make an effort to engage with them. This can create a self-fulfilling prophecy, where the other person becomes even more unfriendly because they feel rejected or ignored. Conversely, if we perceive someone as being friendly and approachable, we are more likely to initiate conversation or social interaction with them, which can lead to a positive relationship.

It's also important to note that our perceptions of others are not always accurate or fair. We may make assumptions or judgments based on limited information or past experiences, which can be biased or incorrect. This is why it's essential to be aware of our perceptions and challenge them when necessary to avoid negative impacts on our relationships.

In a relationship, the impact of perception can be even more significant. Our perception of our partner can influence our level of trust, intimacy, and overall satisfaction in the relationship. If we perceive our partner as being untrustworthy or uncaring, it can create a rift in the relationship that is difficult to overcome.

Therefore, it's important to work on developing a realistic and positive perception of our partner. This means being aware of our own biases and assumptions and actively seeking out information and experiences that can challenge them. It also means communicating with our partner and listening to their perspective to gain a more complete and accurate perception of them.

In summary, our perception of others can have a significant impact on our behavior towards them, and in a relationship, it can influence our level of trust, intimacy, and overall satisfaction. It's essential to be aware of our perceptions and challenge them when necessary to avoid negative impacts on our relationships.

Techniques for improving relationships through perception management

Perception plays a crucial role in the dynamics of our relationships, as the way we perceive others can influence how we behave towards them. In order to improve our relationships with others, it is important to be aware of our perceptions and how they may be affecting our interactions.

One technique for improving relationships through perception management is to practice empathy. Empathy involves putting ourselves in the other person's shoes and trying to see the situation from their perspective. This can help us understand their behavior and motivations, which can in turn help us communicate more effectively and respond in a more positive way.

Another technique is to practice active listening. Active listening involves giving our full attention to the other person, without judgment or interruption. This allows us to better understand their point of view and communicate more effectively, leading to more positive interactions.

It is also important to be aware of our own biases and assumptions, and to challenge them when necessary. For example, if we have a negative perception of someone based on past experiences, we may be more likely to interpret their actions in a negative light, even if they have no intention of causing harm. By recognizing these biases and consciously trying to see the situation objectively, we can avoid misunderstandings and improve our relationships.

It can also be helpful to communicate openly and honestly with others about our perceptions and how they may be affecting our interactions. By expressing our thoughts and feelings in a non-judgmental way, we can create a more positive and respectful dialogue, which can lead to better relationships.

Techniques for improving relationships through perception management involve becoming more aware of how our perceptions shape our thoughts, feelings, and behavior towards others. By recognizing and addressing our biases and assumptions, we can improve our relationships and communication with others.

One such technique is active listening. Active listening involves focusing on what the other person is saying, asking clarifying questions, and reflecting back what we have heard to confirm understanding. This technique can help improve communication and prevent misunderstandings that may result from faulty perceptions.

Another technique is perspective-taking. Perspective-taking involves putting ourselves in the other person's shoes and trying to see things from their point of view. By doing this, we can gain a deeper understanding of their perspective and motivations, and reduce the likelihood of negative assumptions or judgments.

A third technique is mindfulness. Mindfulness involves being present in the moment and aware of our thoughts, feelings, and bodily sensations. By practicing mindfulness, we can become more aware of our own biases and assumptions and learn to recognize and manage them in our relationships with others.

For example, let's say you have a coworker who is always interrupting you in meetings. Your perception may be that they are rude and disrespectful, and this may cause you to feel frustrated and resentful towards them. By actively listening to their comments, perspective-taking to understand their motivations, and practicing mindfulness to manage your own biases and assumptions, you may discover that they are not intentionally trying to be rude, but may have a different communication style or may be enthusiastic about the topic being discussed. This new understanding can lead to a more positive and productive relationship with your coworker.

Overall, by using perception management techniques, we can improve our relationships with others, reduce misunderstandings, and build stronger, more positive connections.

Finally, it is important to remember that perceptions can be changed over time through experiences and learning. By being open to new information and perspectives, we can challenge our assumptions and develop a more positive outlook, leading to more fulfilling and positive relationships.

VIII

Perception and Creativity

Creativity is a valuable skill in all areas of life, from business and science to the arts and personal development. The ability to see things in a new light and approach problems in innovative ways is essential for progress and success. In this chapter, we will explore the relationship between perception and creativity, how perception affects creativity, and how we can use perception to enhance our creative thinking.

The relationship between perception and creativity:

Perception is a critical component of creativity. Creative thinking involves looking at things from different angles and making connections between seemingly unrelated concepts. Perception allows us to see things in new ways, recognize patterns, and form new ideas based on our observations.

Research has shown that people with high levels of creativity have a more flexible and open-minded approach to perception. They are less constrained by preconceived ideas and more likely to consider unconventional perspectives. By being open to new ideas and different perspectives, they can make connections between seemingly unrelated concepts and generate unique and innovative ideas.

The impact of perception on creativity:

Perception can impact creativity in several ways. For example, our perceptions of ourselves, our abilities, and our potential can impact our creativity. If we have a negative self-image or believe that we are not creative, we may limit ourselves and not explore our creative potential fully. On the other hand, if we have a positive perception of ourselves and our abilities, we are more likely to take risks, try new things, and approach problems with an open mind.

Similarly, our perceptions of the world around us can impact our creativity. If we are surrounded by a familiar environment and routine, we may find it challenging to come up with new ideas. However, if we can see our environment in a new light or explore new places, we may find ourselves inspired by the new experiences, leading to creative insights.

Techniques for using perception to enhance creativity:

Perspective-taking:

To generate new ideas, it is crucial to view things from different angles. By putting yourself in someone else's shoes, you can gain a new perspective and find a new solution to the problem. For example, if you are trying to create a marketing campaign for a product, try to imagine what it would be like to be a customer and think about what would appeal to you.

Open-mindedness:

Being open-minded means being willing to consider different perspectives and ideas. Instead of shutting down an idea, take the time to explore it and see where it leads. You may be surprised by the innovative solutions that arise.

Curiosity:

Curiosity is a driving force in creative thinking. By staying curious about the world around you, you can discover new information, identify patterns, and generate new ideas. Be curious about everything from everyday experiences to big-picture concepts and explore them in-depth.

Mindfulness:

Mindfulness involves being fully present in the moment, without judgment or distraction. By practicing mindfulness, you can become more aware of your thoughts and perceptions, allowing you to recognize and challenge preconceived ideas that may limit your creativity.

Perception plays a crucial role in creative thinking. By being open to new perspectives, exploring different angles, and challenging preconceived ideas, we can unlock our creative potential and generate innovative ideas. By using the techniques discussed in this chapter, we can improve our perception and enhance our creative thinking in all areas of life.

How perception affects creativity and innovation

Perception plays a critical role in the way we approach creative tasks and generate new ideas. Our perceptions of the world around us can either enhance or limit our ability to think creatively and come up with innovative solutions.

One way in which perception affects creativity is through our ability to see things from a different perspective. When we approach a problem with a fresh perspective, we may be able to identify new connections or opportunities that we may have otherwise missed.

For example, someone who is used to seeing a particular object in a certain way may struggle to come up with creative uses for that object. However, if they can shift their perception of the object and see it in a new light, they may be able to generate new and innovative ideas.

Another way in which perception affects creativity is through our ability to recognize patterns and make connections between seemingly disparate ideas. This is known as "divergent thinking," and it involves looking at a problem or concept from multiple angles and exploring different possibilities.

For example, an artist may use their perception to see patterns and connections in their surroundings, which they can then use to create unique and interesting artwork.

On the other hand, certain perceptions and beliefs can also limit our creativity. For instance, if we have preconceived notions or biases, we may fail to see opportunities or possibilities that don't fit within our established worldview. Additionally, we may be influenced by the perceptions of others, such as societal norms or cultural expectations, which may constrain our thinking and limit our creativity.

Perception plays a significant role in shaping creativity and innovation. It involves interpreting the information gathered from the environment and using it to generate new ideas or solutions. In this sense, our perception of the world determines the scope of our creative potential.

One way that perception affects creativity is through the way we approach problems. When we have a limited perception of a problem, we tend to solve it in a conventional manner. However, by broadening our perception, we can discover new perspectives and find more innovative solutions.

For example, consider a company facing a marketing challenge. The conventional approach may be to use traditional advertising techniques, but a broader perception may lead to the discovery of a new target market or a unique approach to the product's features that can differentiate it from competitors.

Another way perception affects creativity is by shaping the way we interact with our environment. By being open to new experiences and perspectives, we can broaden our perception, which can enhance creativity. Conversely, a narrow perception may restrict our creative potential.

For example, an artist who is only familiar with one style of painting may have limited creative potential, while an artist who explores different styles and techniques can broaden their perception and generate more innovative artwork.

Moreover, perception can affect creativity by influencing how we perceive risks and challenges. A negative perception of risks and challenges can restrict creative potential, while a positive perception can inspire and motivate us to find innovative solutions.

For instance, a startup entrepreneur who perceives obstacles as opportunities to learn and grow can find more innovative ways to solve problems and develop creative solutions.

Overall, perception plays a significant role in shaping creativity and innovation. By broadening our perception and adopting a positive attitude towards risks and challenges, we can unlock our creative potential and generate more innovative solutions.

Techniques for enhancing creativity through perception awareness

There are many techniques that can be used to enhance creativity through perception awareness. Here are a few examples:

Mind Mapping:

Mind mapping is a technique that can be used to help generate new ideas and connections between existing ideas. It involves creating a visual map of a topic or problem, using images, words, and colors to represent different ideas and concepts. This technique can help to break down complex ideas into more manageable pieces, and to identify new connections and relationships that might not have been apparent before.

For example, if you were trying to come up with a new marketing campaign for a product, you might create a mind map with the product at the center, and branches leading out to different marketing strategies and ideas.

Re-framing:

Re-framing involves looking at a problem or situation from a different perspective, in order to identify new solutions or opportunities. This technique can be particularly useful when trying to break out of established patterns of thinking or behavior.

For example, if you were trying to come up with a new product design, you might try re-framing the problem by looking at it from the perspective of a different user group, or by focusing on a different aspect of the product.

Divergent Thinking: Divergent thinking involves generating multiple ideas and solutions to a problem, rather than focusing on a single "correct" answer. This can help to open up new possibilities and avenues for exploration, and to generate more creative and innovative solutions.

For example, if you were trying to come up with a new feature for a software application, you might brainstorm a list of 50 different ideas, without worrying about whether they are all feasible or practical.

Sensory Exploration: Sensory exploration involves using different senses and perspectives to gain new insights and ideas. This can involve experimenting with different materials, textures, and colors, or using different senses such as touch, smell, or taste to explore a problem or idea.

For example, if you were trying to come up with a new design for a product packaging, you might experiment with different textures and materials to create a more tactile and engaging experience for the customer.

By using these and other techniques, it is possible to enhance creativity and innovation through perception awareness, and to break out of established patterns of thinking and behavior.

IX

Perception and Mindfulness

In this chapter, we will explore the relationship between perception and mindfulness. Mindfulness is the practice of being present and fully engaged in the current moment, and it can have a profound impact on our perception of the world around us. By learning to cultivate mindfulness, we can become more attuned to our own perceptions and the experiences that shape them, leading to greater clarity, peace, and fulfillment in life.

The Practice of Mindfulness

At its core, mindfulness is about learning to be fully present and engaged in the current moment, without judgment or distraction. This can involve a variety of practices, such as meditation, deep breathing, or mindful movement, but the basic idea is the same: to cultivate a state of awareness and presence that allows us to fully engage with our own thoughts, emotions, and experiences.

Through mindfulness practice, we can begin to notice the subtle ways in which our perceptions are shaped by our thoughts, feelings, and physical sensations. By developing greater awareness of these factors, we can learn to separate them from the raw data of our perceptions, and begin to see the world more clearly and objectively.

The Impact of Mindfulness on Perception

When we learn to approach our perceptions with greater awareness and presence, we can begin to see the world in a more open, flexible, and compassionate way. This can help us to break down the rigid, fixed patterns of thinking that can sometimes keep us stuck in unproductive or negative mindsets.

By practicing mindfulness, we can also become more attuned to the subtle nuances of our own perceptions, and the ways in which they are shaped by our own thoughts, feelings, and beliefs. This can help us to recognize and overcome cognitive biases and other distortions that may be clouding our judgment or limiting our potential.

Techniques for Cultivating Mindfulness

There are many different techniques and practices that can help us cultivate mindfulness and enhance our perception of the world around us. Some common techniques include:

Mindful Breathing:

Focusing on the sensations of the breath as it enters and leaves the body, and learning to let go of distracting thoughts and sensations.

Body Scan:

Bringing awareness to the physical sensations of different parts of the body, from the toes to the head, and cultivating a sense of relaxation and openness.

Loving Kindness Meditation:

Cultivating feelings of warmth, compassion, and connection towards ourselves and others, and learning to see the world through a lens of kindness and generosity.

By practicing these and other mindfulness techniques, we can begin to cultivate greater awareness, presence, and insight into our own perceptions, and the world around us. Over time, this can lead to greater creativity, fulfillment, and happiness in our lives, as we learn to see the world more clearly and compassionately, and to engage with it in a more meaningful and productive way.

The role of perception in mindfulness and meditation

Perception plays a crucial role in mindfulness and meditation. These practices aim to develop a deeper awareness and understanding of our thoughts, emotions, and sensations, and perception is the way we interpret and make sense of these experiences.

Mindfulness involves paying attention to the present moment with a non-judgmental attitude. Perception influences how we perceive the world around us and how we interpret our experiences. Therefore, being aware of our perception can help us to be more mindful and present in the moment.

Meditation is a form of mindfulness practice that involves focusing on a particular object, thought, or activity to train the mind to be more aware and focused. Perception can affect the way we experience and interpret the object of meditation. By being aware of our perceptions, we can better understand and work with our thoughts and emotions during meditation.

For example, suppose we are meditating on our breath. Our perception of our breath can impact the quality of our meditation practice. If we perceive our breath as shallow or difficult to control, we may become anxious or frustrated. However, if we perceive our breath as calm and soothing, we may feel more relaxed and focused.

By being aware of our perceptions during mindfulness and meditation practices, we can develop a deeper understanding of our thoughts, emotions, and sensations. We can observe them without judgment, accept them for what they are, and let them pass without getting caught up in them.

The practice of mindfulness and meditation involves developing awareness of one's thoughts, feelings, and physical sensations in the present moment. Perception plays a crucial role in this process, as it shapes our experience of the world around us and influences the quality of our thoughts and emotions.

By cultivating a non-judgmental awareness of our perceptions, we can begin to identify habitual patterns of thinking and feeling that may be causing us distress or limiting our potential. For example, if we tend to perceive ourselves as inadequate or unworthy, this belief may contribute to feelings of anxiety, depression, or low self-esteem. By bringing mindful attention to these patterns, we can begin to challenge them and develop new, more positive perceptions of ourselves and the world around us.

Similarly, our perceptions of others can also impact our ability to be present and attentive in relationships. By becoming more aware of our own biases and preconceptions, we can learn to approach others with greater openness and empathy, leading to deeper and more meaningful connections.

Practicing mindfulness and meditation can also help us to develop a more expansive and flexible perception of reality. By learning to observe our thoughts and feelings without judgment or attachment, we can become more attuned to the nuances of our own experience and the world around us. This heightened sensitivity can lead to increased creativity, problem-solving ability, and overall sense of well-being.

There are many techniques and practices that can be used to enhance perception and mindfulness, such as meditation, breathwork, and body awareness exercises. By incorporating these practices into our daily lives, we can learn to cultivate a more present and open-minded approach to the world around us, leading to greater peace, happiness, and fulfillment.

Overall, perception is a vital component of mindfulness and meditation practices. Being aware of our perceptions can help us to cultivate a deeper sense of mindfulness and inner peace.

Techniques for improving mindfulness through perception awareness

There are various techniques for improving mindfulness through perception awareness. Here are a few examples:

Body scan:

Body scan is a mindfulness technique that involves paying attention to different parts of the body, one at a time. By focusing on the sensations in each part of the body, one can become more aware of their bodily experience and develop greater mindfulness.

Breath awareness:

Breath awareness is another mindfulness technique that involves paying attention to the breath as it enters and leaves the body. By focusing on the breath, one can develop greater awareness of their thoughts and emotions, and learn to observe them without getting caught up in them.

Open monitoring:

Open monitoring is a mindfulness technique that involves observing one's thoughts and emotions without judgment. By cultivating an attitude of non-judgmental awareness, one can learn to let go of negative thoughts and emotions, and focus on the present moment.

Loving-kindness meditation:

Loving-kindness meditation is a mindfulness technique that involves cultivating feelings of compassion and kindness towards oneself and others. By focusing on positive emotions, one can cultivate greater mindfulness and reduce negative thoughts and emotions.

Mindful walking:

Mindful walking involves paying attention to the sensations in the feet and body as one walks. By focusing on the present moment, one can develop greater awareness and mindfulness in their daily life.

These techniques can be practiced in a variety of settings, such as during a meditation session, while doing daily tasks, or during a walk in nature. By incorporating these techniques into one's daily routine, one can develop greater perception awareness and improve their overall well-being.

X

Perception and Health

Perception plays a critical role in our overall health and well-being. It influences how we interpret and respond to various health-related situations, and can even impact our physical health. This chapter will explore the relationship between perception and health, and how we can utilize perception to promote a healthier and more balanced lifestyle.

The Impact of Perception on Health:

Our perception of health and illness can greatly impact our overall well-being. The way we perceive our own health, as well as the health of others, can influence our behaviors, emotions, and even our physical health outcomes. For example, if we perceive our health negatively, we may experience more stress and anxiety, which can lead to physical symptoms like headaches, muscle tension, and sleep disturbances.

On the other hand, if we have a positive perception of health, we are more likely to engage in healthy behaviors, such as exercise and a balanced diet, which can lead to improved physical health outcomes. Our perception can also impact our ability to cope with illness and injury, as well as our overall quality of life.

Perception and Chronic Illness:

For individuals with chronic illness, perception can play an even more significant role in their overall well-being. The way we perceive our illness can influence our ability to manage symptoms and engage in self-care behaviors. For example, if we perceive our illness as a personal failure or weakness, we may be less likely to engage in self-care behaviors or seek treatment.

Alternatively, if we view our illness as a challenge to be overcome, we may be more likely to take an active role in our care and engage in behaviors that promote health and well-being. Additionally, perception can influence how we cope with symptoms and the emotional impact of illness.

Perception and Healthcare:

Perception also plays a critical role in the healthcare system. The way we perceive healthcare providers, treatment options, and the overall healthcare system can impact our willingness to seek care and engage in treatment.

For example, if we perceive healthcare providers as judgmental or dismissive, we may be less likely to seek care or follow recommended treatment plans.

Alternatively, if we perceive our healthcare providers as supportive and compassionate, we may be more likely to engage in treatment and experience better health outcomes. Our perception can also influence our adherence to medication regimens and other treatment plans.

Techniques for Improving Health through Perception Management:

There are several techniques for improving health through perception management. One of the most effective is mindfulness, which involves focusing our attention on the present moment and accepting our experiences without judgment. Mindfulness can help us develop a more positive perception of our health, reduce stress and anxiety, and improve our overall well-being.

Another technique is cognitive restructuring, which involves identifying and challenging negative thought patterns that may be impacting our health behaviors and outcomes. By replacing negative thoughts with more positive and realistic ones, we can improve our perception of health and engage in healthier behaviors.

In conclusion, our perception plays a significant role in our overall health and well-being. By developing a more positive and realistic perception of health, we can improve our behaviors, emotions, and physical health outcomes. Through techniques like mindfulness and cognitive restructuring, we can improve our perception and promote a healthier and more balanced lifestyle.

The impact of perception on health and well-being

Perception can have a significant impact on our health and well-being. Our beliefs, attitudes, and expectations can shape our experiences and influence our physical and mental health. For example, if someone believes that they are prone to illness, they may experience more symptoms of illness than someone who believes they are generally healthy.

Perception can also play a role in the placebo effect, which is when a person experiences a positive health outcome after receiving a treatment that is not medically effective. This effect is believed to be the result of the patient's belief that the treatment will be effective, which can trigger the body's natural healing processes.

Additionally, negative perceptions and stress can contribute to a range of health problems, including high blood pressure, heart disease, and mental health issues. On the other hand, positive perceptions and a sense of optimism can contribute to better health outcomes and a stronger immune system.

For example, studies have found that people with positive perceptions of aging tend to live longer and experience better health in their later years. Similarly, people who have a positive perception of their own abilities to cope with stress tend to experience less stress-related illnesses.

In sum, our perceptions can play a significant role in our overall health and well-being. By being aware of our perceptions and working to shift negative beliefs and attitudes, we can improve our physical and mental health.

Techniques for using perception to improve physical and mental health

Our perception can have a significant impact on our physical and mental health. By shifting our perception, we can improve our well-being and reduce stress and anxiety.

One technique for using perception to improve physical health is visualization. Visualization is a mental imagery technique that can be used to promote relaxation and healing. By imagining positive outcomes and focusing on healing imagery, people can reduce stress and promote healing.

For example, a person with chronic pain can visualize the pain decreasing and the affected area healing.

Another technique for using perception to improve mental health is reframing. Reframing is a cognitive technique that involves changing the way we think about a situation. By changing the way we perceive a situation, we can change our emotional response and reduce stress and anxiety.

For example, instead of viewing a difficult situation as a failure, we can reframe it as a learning opportunity.

Meditation is another technique that can be used to improve mental health through perception. By focusing on the present moment and accepting thoughts without judgment, people can reduce stress and improve their well-being. Studies have shown that regular meditation can improve symptoms of depression and anxiety.

Finally, mindful eating is a technique that can be used to improve physical and mental health. By focusing on the taste, texture, and smell of food, people can slow down and savor their food. Mindful eating can reduce stress and promote a healthy relationship with food.

XI

Perception and Success

Perception and success are intricately linked. The way we perceive ourselves, others, and the world around us can have a significant impact on our ability to achieve our goals and realize our full potential. Perception is not just about what we see or hear; it is also about how we interpret and make meaning out of the information we receive. In this chapter, we will explore how perception influences success and what strategies can be used to improve our perception for greater success. We will also examine how individuals with different perspectives and backgrounds can leverage their unique perceptions to achieve their goals.

Success is a subjective term that means different things to different people. However, one thing that remains constant is that success requires a certain level of perception, specifically, the ability to accurately interpret one's environment and make informed decisions. In this chapter, we will explore how perception can influence our success and the techniques for improving perception to achieve success.

The Role of Perception in Success:

Perception plays a vital role in success. The ability to perceive, process, and analyze information is critical in making informed decisions, solving problems, and taking advantage of opportunities. Perception allows us to understand the complex world around us, and it helps us to filter information and make sense of it. Successful people are generally those who are good at making sense of their environment and making informed decisions based on the information they perceive.

The Impact of Perception on Success:

Perception can have a significant impact on success. A person's perception of their abilities, resources, and opportunities can either facilitate or hinder success. For instance, if someone perceives themselves as inadequate and incompetent, they are likely to miss opportunities and lack the confidence to pursue success. Conversely, those who perceive themselves as capable and resourceful are more likely to take advantage of opportunities and succeed.

Techniques for Improving Perception for Success:

Perception is a learnable skill that can be developed and improved. Here are some techniques for improving perception to achieve success:

Mindfulness:

Mindfulness is a technique that involves paying attention to the present moment, including one's thoughts and feelings, without judgment. Practicing mindfulness can help improve perception by enabling a person to notice more details about their environment and make more informed decisions.

Visualization:

Visualization is a technique that involves creating a mental image of a desired outcome. By visualizing success, one can develop a positive perception of their abilities, opportunities, and resources, which can boost their confidence and motivation to succeed.

Challenging Cognitive Biases:

Cognitive biases are mental shortcuts that can lead to inaccurate perceptions and judgments. By recognizing and challenging these biases, one can develop a more accurate and informed perception of their environment.

Building Resilience:

Resilience is the ability to adapt to change, overcome challenges, and bounce back from setbacks. Building resilience can help improve perception by enabling a person to view setbacks and challenges as opportunities for growth rather than as obstacles to success.

Seeking Feedback:

Seeking feedback from others can help improve perception by providing a different perspective on one's abilities, strengths, and weaknesses. This can help identify areas for improvement and facilitate personal growth.

In conclusion, perception is an essential factor in success. Developing a positive and accurate perception of oneself, one's environment, and one's opportunities is critical to achieving success. By using the techniques outlined above, individuals can improve their perception and enhance their chances of success in all areas of life.

The relationship between perception and success

The relationship between perception and success is a complex one. Our perceptions of ourselves, our abilities, and the world around us can have a profound impact on our level of success in various aspects of life.

For example, if someone perceives themselves as capable, confident, and competent, they may be more likely to take risks, pursue opportunities, and achieve their goals.

On the other hand, if someone perceives themselves as limited, unworthy, or inadequate, they may be more likely to shy away from challenges, give up on their goals, and settle for less than they deserve. This illustrates how our perception of ourselves can have a significant impact on our level of success.

Perception can also impact our success in social and professional settings. For instance, people who are perceptive and socially aware are more likely to be successful in forming and maintaining positive relationships. They can read the emotions and body language of others, communicate more effectively, and respond appropriately to various social situations.

Moreover, in the professional world, perception plays a crucial role in determining success. People who perceive themselves and their colleagues in a positive light and maintain an optimistic outlook are more likely to be successful. They are likely to be viewed as capable and confident, and they are more likely to be given challenging tasks and opportunities for growth.

For example, if two employees with similar qualifications and experience are up for a promotion, the one who has a more positive perception of themselves and their abilities may be more likely to get the job. This is because they may be more likely to project confidence during the interview and have a more optimistic outlook, which could make them seem like a better fit for the role.

In conclusion, perception plays a critical role in determining our level of success. Our perception of ourselves, others, and the world around us can impact our confidence, decision-making, communication, and actions. Hence, it is essential to have a positive and accurate perception to maximize our chances of success in various aspects of life.

Techniques for enhancing success through perception management

Perception plays an important role in determining our success in various areas of life, including career, relationships, and personal growth. By becoming aware of how our perception shapes our thoughts and actions, we can take control of our lives and achieve our goals more effectively.

Here are some techniques for enhancing success through perception management:

Positive visualization:

Visualizing ourselves succeeding in our goals can have a powerful effect on our perception and mindset. By creating mental images of success, we can program our brains to perceive and act in ways that will lead to the desired outcomes.

For example, an athlete who visualizes winning a race may become more motivated and focused during training, leading to better performance.

Self-talk:

Our internal dialogue can greatly affect our perception and behavior. By cultivating positive self-talk and reframing negative thoughts, we can create a more supportive and empowering perception of ourselves and our abilities.

or example, instead of saying "I'm not good enough," we can say "I am capable of learning and improving."

Mindfulness:

Being mindful and present in the moment can help us tune into our perception and become more aware of our thoughts and feelings. By noticing and acknowledging negative or limiting beliefs, we can work to reframe them and create a more positive perception.

Mindfulness practices such as meditation and deep breathing can help to reduce stress and improve focus, leading to better decision-making and more success.

Seeking out diverse perspectives:

Our perception can be limited by our own experiences and biases. By actively seeking out diverse perspectives and learning from people with different backgrounds and viewpoints, we can broaden our perception and gain new insights and ideas. This can lead to more creative problem-solving and better decision-making, ultimately leading to greater success.

Embracing failure:

Our perception of failure can greatly affect our willingness to take risks and pursue success. By reframing failure as an opportunity for growth and learning, we can overcome our fear of failure and become more resilient and persistent in our pursuit of success.

For example, a business owner who sees failure as a learning experience may be more willing to take risks and try new strategies, ultimately leading to greater success.

Overall, by becoming more aware of how our perception affects our thoughts and actions, we can take control of our lives and achieve greater success in all areas.

XII
Perception and the Future

The future is always uncertain, but our perceptions of it can shape the actions we take in the present to create the future we desire. Perception is a critical factor in how we think about the future, and it can play a significant role in our ability to plan, prepare, and take action.

Perception of the Future

Our perception of the future is often colored by our past experiences, biases, and expectations. How we perceive the future can have a significant impact on our present actions and can determine whether we take action or not. Our perception of the future can be influenced by a variety of factors, including our environment, culture, social norms, media, and personal beliefs.

For example, someone who has experienced financial struggles in the past may perceive the future as being financially uncertain, even if they have taken steps to improve their financial situation. This perception can lead to anxiety and inaction, preventing them from taking the necessary steps to build a more financially secure future.

Similarly, someone who has experienced success in the past may have a more positive perception of the future, leading them to take more risks and be more proactive in pursuing their goals.

Perception and Action

Our perception of the future can have a significant impact on our actions and behavior in the present. How we perceive the future can determine whether we take risks or play it safe, whether we pursue our goals or settle for what we have.

For example, if we perceive the future as being uncertain or risky, we may be more hesitant to take action or pursue our goals. On the other hand, if we perceive the future as being full of opportunities and potential, we may be more willing to take risks and pursue our dreams.

Perception and Planning

Our perception of the future is also critical in how we plan for it. How we perceive the future can determine whether we plan for it or not and can affect the types of plans we make.

For example, someone who perceives the future as being unpredictable or unstable may be less likely to plan for it, leading to a lack of preparation and increased vulnerability to unexpected events. On the other hand, someone who perceives the future as being relatively stable and predictable may be more likely to plan for it, leading to increased preparedness and resilience.

Techniques for Managing Perception and the Future

Managing our perception of the future is critical in achieving our goals and creating the future we desire. Here are some techniques that can help us manage our perception of the future:

Visualization:

Visualization is a technique that involves visualizing a desired future outcome. By creating a mental picture of what we want to achieve, we can begin to shift our perception of the future and focus on the steps we need to take to achieve our goals.

Goal setting:

Setting clear, achievable goals can help us manage our perception of the future by breaking it down into manageable steps.

By setting specific goals and creating a plan for achieving them, we can begin to shift our perception of the future from being uncertain or overwhelming to being achievable and within our control.

Mindfulness:

Mindfulness is a technique that involves being present and fully engaged in the moment. By practicing mindfulness, we can become more aware of our thoughts and feelings and begin to shift our perception of the future from being uncertain or unpredictable to being full of possibilities.

Positive self-talk:

Positive self-talk involves using positive language and affirmations to shift our perception of the future. By focusing on positive outcomes and using positive language, we can begin to shift our perception of the future from being negative or uncertain to being positive and hopeful.

Perception is a critical factor in how we think about the future and can play a significant role in our ability to plan, prepare, and take action. By managing our perception of the future

The future of perception and its impact on technology and society

The future of perception promises to bring about revolutionary changes in technology and society. Advances in technology will likely lead to new ways of perceiving and interacting with the world around us. One area where this is already happening is virtual and augmented reality, where users can be transported to entirely different environments and experience them as if they were real.

For example, virtual reality is being used to simulate medical procedures, allowing doctors to practice complex surgeries in a safe and controlled environment before performing them on real patients. This has the potential to improve patient outcomes and reduce medical errors.

Another example is in the field of education, where virtual and augmented reality can be used to provide immersive learning experiences that can engage students and improve their retention of information. Students can explore historical sites, scientific phenomena, or other parts of the world from their classrooms, providing a new level of educational access.

In the world of entertainment, new forms of media such as 360-degree videos and interactive experiences are being developed to give viewers a more immersive and engaging experience. This can be seen in the rise of interactive movie experiences, where viewers can make choices that affect the outcome of the story.

However, with these advances come challenges related to privacy, ethics, and the potential for addiction or over-reliance on technology. As the boundaries between reality and virtual reality become increasingly blurred, individuals may struggle to distinguish between what is real and what is not, leading to a distorted perception of the world.

Moreover, as technology continues to shape our lives, the impact of social media on perception and communication will likely continue to evolve. The growing use of social media platforms has given rise to a new form of influence, with online personalities and influencers playing an increasingly important role in shaping public opinion and perception. This has both positive and negative consequences, as it can create new opportunities for engagement and education, but also foster echo chambers and misinformation.

In conclusion, the future of perception holds tremendous potential for transformative change. Advances in technology and new ways of perceiving the world will continue to shape society in ways that are difficult to predict. It is important to remain aware of the opportunities and challenges that arise from these developments, and to use our perception as a tool for growth and positive change.

Opportunities and challenges for perception management in the future

As technology and society continue to evolve, the field of perception management faces both opportunities and challenges.

One opportunity for perception management lies in the realm of virtual and augmented reality. With the increasing prevalence of these technologies, there will be new opportunities to manage and manipulate perception in immersive environments. For example, virtual reality therapy is already being used to treat anxiety disorders by immersing patients in virtual scenarios that trigger their fears and allow them to gradually overcome them.

Another opportunity for perception management is the growing awareness of cognitive biases and heuristics, which has led to the development of tools and techniques for recognizing and counteracting these biases. For example, some companies are using algorithms to help reduce bias in hiring processes, and there are apps and tools available to help individuals recognize and counteract their own biases.

However, there are also challenges to perception management in the future. One challenge is the increasing sophistication of fake news and propaganda. With advances in technology, it is becoming easier to create convincing fake videos and images, making it more difficult for individuals to discern what is true and what is not. This can have significant implications for politics, public health, and more.

Another challenge is the potential for privacy violations as technology increasingly collects data on individuals‘ behaviors and preferences. As perception management becomes more sophisticated, it is important to ensure that individuals' privacy is protected and that their personal information is not used against them.

In summary, the future of perception management presents both opportunities and challenges. As technology continues to evolve, there will be new opportunities to use perception management to improve physical and mental health, enhance creativity, and improve decision making. However, there are also risks and challenges associated with the increasing sophistication of fake news and propaganda, and the need to protect individuals' privacy as more data is collected and analyzed. It is up to individuals, organizations, and society as a whole to navigate these opportunities and challenges in a way that maximizes the benefits of perception management while minimizing the risks.

Famous Quotes About Perception

I have gathered well-known quotes about perception that could offer you new insights.

1. "Perception precedes reality." - Andy Warhol.
2. "The more I see, the less I know for sure." - John Lennon.
3. "It's all in the mind." - George Harrison.
4. "There is nothing either good or bad, but thinking makes it so." - William Shakespeare.
5. "Your perception may not be my reality." - Aporva Kala.
6. "A work of art doesn't exist outside the perception of the audience." - Abbas Kiarostami.
7. "All our knowledge has its origins in our perceptions." - Leonardo da Vinci.
8. "What we observe is not nature itself, but nature exposed to our method of questioning." - Werner Heisenberg.
9. "Perceptions about people can be powerful. They can also be powerfully wrong." - Craig Dresang.
10. "Perception is created and twisted so quickly." - Louis C. K.
11. "Intuition comes very close to clairvoyance; it appears to be the extrasensory perception of reality." - Alexis Carrel.
12. "It was the best of times, it was the worst of times." - Charles Dickens.
13. "Trust in yourself. Your perceptions are often far more accurate than you are willing to believe." - Claudia Black.
14. "Life is 10 percent what you make it, and 90 percent how you take it." - Irving Berlin.
15. "Some people see the cup as half empty. Some people see the cup as half full. I see the cup as too large." - George Carlin.
16. "The only thing that makes life unfair is the delusion that it should be fair." - Steve Maraboli.
17. "I believe I am in Hell; therefore I am." - Arthur Rimbaud.
18. "Everything that irritates us about others can lead us to an understanding of ourselves." - Carl Jung.

19. "Speak up, stand up, and keep correcting the false perceptions. Stay true to your heart's views and keep chanting for peace and justice." - Suzy Kassem.

20. "Change the way you look at things and the things you look at change." - Wayne W. Dyer.

21. "Every exit is an entry somewhere." - Tom Stoppard.

22. "Be thankful for what you have; you'll end up having more. If you concentrate on what you don't have, you will never, ever have enough." - Oprah Winfrey.

23. "What people in the world think of you is really none of your business." - Martha Graham.

24. "If the doors of perception were cleansed, everything would appear as it is – infinite." - William Blake.

25. "Your perception of the world is not necessarily the same as what is actually occurring." - Peter Ralston.

26. "There is a major ingredient missing from our perception of how changes are brought about; that ingredient is power." - Paul Wellstone.

27. "There are always two people in every picture: the photographer and the viewer." - Ansel Adams.

28. "To change ourselves effectively, we first had to change our perceptions." - Stephen R. Covey.

29. "Just remember that sometimes the way you think about a person isn't the way they actually are." - John Green.

30. "Better keep yourself clean and bright; you are the window through which you must see the world." - George Bernard Shaw.

31. "The moment you change your perception is the moment you rewrite the chemistry of your body." - Dr. Bruce Lipton.

32. "Miracles are a shift in perception." - Kenneth Wapnick.

33. "It's not what you look at that matters, it's what you see." - Henry David Thoreau.

34. "What I had to learn was, that I'm responsible for my perception of things." - Chris Robinson.

35. "The world is full of magic things, patiently waiting for our senses to grow sharper." - W.B. Yeats.

36. "Closed in a room, my imagination becomes the universe, and the rest of the world is missing out." - Criss Jami.

37. "If you look at your life one way, there is always cause for alarm." - Elizabeth Bowen.

38. "We have to reshape our own perception of how we view ourselves." - Beyonce.

39. "Facts matter not at all. Perception is everything. It's certainty." - Stephen Colbert.

40. "I think the perception of peace is what distracts most people from really having it." - Joyce Meyer.

41. "Reality is always kinder than the stories we tell about it." - Byron Katie.

42. "Life is all about perception. Positive versus negative. Whichever you choose will affect and more than likely reflect your outcomes." - Sonya Teclai.

43. "The dung beetle, seeing its child on the wall, thinks it sees a pearl on a thread." - Arabic Proverb.

44. "One's perception of themselves has a much bigger role than has been acknowledged to determine who succeeds and who does not." - Sal Khan.

45. "All our knowledge is the offspring of our perceptions." - Leonardo Di Vinci.

46. "Our vulgar perception is not concerned with other than vulgar phenomena." - Samuel Beckett.

47. "The problem is not our situation but our perception of our situation." - Graham Cooke.

48. "Your perception creates your reality. You can look at life and see scarcity or abundance. It depends on your mindset." - Joe Vitale.

49. "Silently hear everyone. Accept what is good. Reject and forget what is not. This is intelligent living." - Chinmayananda Saraswati.

50. "Perception is reality. If you are perceived to be something, you might as well be it because that's the truth in people's minds." - Stever Young.

51. "Death is not extinguishing the light; it is only putting out the lamp because the dawn has come." - Rabindranath Tagore.

52. "Men are disturbed not by things, but by the view which they take of them." - Epictetus.

53. "Reject your sense of injury and the injury itself disappears." - Marcus Aurelius, 'Meditations'.

54. "That is certainly one way to look at the matter. There are others." - Patricia C. Wrede.

55. "We are all in the gutter, but some of us are looking at the stars." - Oscar Wilde, 'Lady Windermere's Fan'.

56. "What you see and what you hear depends a great deal on where you are standing. It also depends on what sort of person you are." - C.S. Lewis.

57. "The most perfidious way of harming a cause consists of defending it deliberately with faulty arguments." - Friedrich Nietzsche.

58. "The clearsighted do not rule the world, but they sustain and console it." - Agnes Repplier.

59. "Only in quiet waters do things mirror themselves undistorted. Only in a quiet mind is adequate perception of the world." - Hans Margolius.

60. "I view it as perception is reality. That means that depends on who's perceiving your reality. We'll leave it at that." - Jose Canseco.

61. "The auditory perception is not sufficient for our knowledge of the world; it does not have vastness." - Robert Delaunay.

62. "People may not tell you how they feel about you, but they always show you. Pay attention." - Keri Hilson.

63. "We must not allow other people's perceptions to define us." - Virginia Satir.

64. "The difference between average people and achieving people is their perception of and response to failure." - John C. Maxwell.

65. "Your agreement with reality defines your life." - Steve Maraboli.

66. "When we become fixed in our perceptions, we lose our ability to fly." - Yongey Mingyur Rinpoche.

67. "Perception is merely reality filtered through the prism of your soul." - Christopher A. Ray.

68. "The last thing a fish would ever notice would be water." - Ralph Linton.

69. "Every man takes the limits of his own field of vision for the limits of the world." - Arthur Schopenhauer, 'Studies In Pessimism: The Essays'.

70. "Everything we see is a perspective, not the truth." - Marcus Aurelius."

71. "Preconceived notions are the locks on the door to wisdom." - Merry Browne.

72. "Most of us have grown up seeing the world as a place of limitation rather than as a place of inexhaustible treasures." - Bob Burg.

73. "If you have an over-preoccupation with perception and trying to please people's expectations, then you can go mad." - Benedict Cumberbatch.

74. "Though we see the same world, we see it through different eyes." - Virginia Woolf.

75. "The universe is change; our life is what our thoughts make it." - Marcus Aurelius.

76. "Songs are as sad as the listener." - Jonathan Safran Foer, 'Extremely Loud & Incredibly Close'.

77. "Most misunderstandings in the world could be avoided if people would simply take the time to ask, 'What else could this mean?'" - Shannon L. Alder.

78. "No life is so hard that you can't make it easier by the way you take it." - Ellen Glasgow.

79. "Where perception is, there also are pain and pleasure, and where these are, there, of necessity, is desire." - Aristotle.

80. "One new perception, one fresh thought, one act of surrender, one change of heart, one leap of faith, can change your life forever." - Robert Holden.

81. "Humans see what they want to see." - Rick Riordan, 'The Lightning Thief'.

82. "All that we see or seem is but a dream within a dream." - Edgar Allen Poe.

83. "Blessed are they who see beautiful things in humble places where other people see nothing." - Camille Pissarro.

84. "With time and experience comes a different perception of what's going on around you." - Chris Robinson.

85. "If I make a fool of myself, who cares? I'm not frightened by anyone's perception of me." - Angelina Jolie.

86. "What is behind your eyes holds more power than what is in front of them." - Gary Zukav.

87. "Everything we hear is an opinion, not a fact." - Marcus Aurelius.

88. "Opting for one perception eliminates all others." - Simone Bingemer.

89. "The voyage of discovery is not in seeking new landscapes but in having new eyes." - Marcel Proust.

90. "Many of the truths we cling to depend greatly on our point of view." - Obi-Wan Kenobi.

91. "Perception is real even when it is not reality." - Edward de Bono.

92. "Always let intuitive perception precede analysis." - Darby Bannard.

93. "Heightened perception is the goal: becoming more aware of how you see, not just what you see." - Michael Kimmelman.

94. "There is an art of seeing things as they are: without naming, without being caught in a network of words, without thinking interfering with perception." - Jiddu Krishnamurti.

95. "Critical perception cannot be imposed." - Paulo Freire.

96. "No perspective, no perception. New perspective, new perception." - Toba Beta.

97. "We think perception is going to become a commodity over the years." - Karl Iagnemma.

98. "We don't see things as they are. We see them as we are." - Anais Nin.

99. "What we see depends mainly on what we look for." - John Lubbock.

100. "Beyond our most stubborn misperception lies often our fondest dream." - Robert Brault.

101. "Every person has a different view of another person's image. That's all perception. The character of a man, the integrity, that's who you are." – Steve Alford

102. "There are things known and there are things unknown, and in between are the doors of perception." – Aldous Huxley

103. "A work of art doesn't exist outside the perception of the audience." – Abbas Kiarostami

104. "We must not allow other people's perceptions to define us." – Virginia Satir

105. "The difference between average people and achieving people is their perception of and response to failure." – John C. Maxwell

106. "If I make a fool of myself, who cares? I'm not frightened by anyone's perception of me." – Angelina Jolie

107. "Life is all about perception. Positive versus negative. Whichever you choose will affect and more than likely reflect your outcomes." – Sonya Teclai

108. "I think the perception of peace is what distracts most people from really having it." – Joyce Meyer

109. "There is no fixed physical reality, no single perception of the world, just numerous ways of interpreting world views as dictated by one's nervous system and the specific environment of our planetary existence." – Deepak Chopra

110. "If the doors of perception were cleansed everything would appear to man as it is, infinite." – William Blake

111. "It's not what you look at that matters, it's what you see." – Henry David Thoreau

112. "The reality of life is that your perceptions – right or wrong – influence everything else you do. When you get a proper

perspective of your perceptions, you may be surprised how many other things fall into place." – Roger Birkman

113. "Miracles are a shift in perception." – Kenneth Wapnick

114. "Speak up, stand up, and keep correcting the false perceptions. Stay true to your hearts views and keep chanting for peace and justice." – Suzy Kassem

115. "Reality doesn't bite, rather our perception of reality bites." – Anthony J. D'Angelo

116. "Your perception creates your reality. You can look at life and see scarcity or abundance. It depends on your mindset." – Joe Vitale

117. "It is above all by the imagination that we achieve perception and compassion and hope." – Ursula K. Le Guin

118. "It used to be, everyone was entitled to their own opinion, but not their own facts. But that's not the case anymore. Facts matter not at all. Perception is everything." – Stephen Colbert

119. "Artists – musicians, painters, writers, poets – always seem to have had the most accurate perception of what is really going on around them, not the official version or the popular perception of contemporary life." – Billy Joel

120. "We are all in the gutter, but some of us are looking at the stars." – Oscar Wilde

121. "The outer world is a reflection of the inner world. Other people's perception of you is a reflection of them; your response to them is an awareness of you." – Roy T. Bennett

122. "There is a major ingredient missing from our perception of how changes are brought about; that ingredient is power." – Paul Wellstone

123. "Because our entire universe is made up of consciousness, we never really experience the universe directly we just experience our consciousness of the universe, our perception of it, so right, our only universe is perception." – Alan Moore

124. "All things are subject to interpretation. Whichever interpretation prevails at a given time is a function of power and not truth." – Friedrich Nietzsche

125. “Intuition comes very close to clairvoyance; it appears to be the extrasensory perception of reality.” – Alexis Carrel

126. “The lunar flights give you a correct perception of our existence. You look back at Earth from the moon, and you can put your thumb up to the window and hide the Earth behind your thumb. Everything you’ve ever known is behind your thumb, and that blue-and-white ball is orbiting a rather normal star, tucked away on the outer edge of a galaxy.” – Jim Lovell

127. “The eye sees only what the mind is prepared to comprehend.” – Robertson Davies

128. “One’s perception of themselves has a much bigger role than has been acknowledged to determine who succeeds and who does not.” – Sal Khan

129. “Maybe each human being lives in a unique world, a private world different from those inhabited and experienced by all other humans. . . If reality differs from person to person, can we speak of reality singular, or shouldn’t we really be talking about plural realities?” – Philip K. Dick

130. “If you have an over-preoccupation with perception and trying to please people’s expectations, then you can go mad.” – Benedict Cumberbatch

131. “No man has the right to dictate what other men should perceive, create or produce, but all should be encouraged to reveal themselves, their perceptions and emotions, and to build confidence in the creative spirit.” – Ansel Adams

132. “What people in the world think of you is really none of your business.” – Martha Graham

133. “Beauty is no quality in things themselves: It exists merely in the mind which contemplates them; and each mind perceives a different beauty.” – David Hume

134. “Because one believes in oneself, one doesn’t try to convince others. Because one is content with oneself, one doesn’t need others’ approval. Because one accepts oneself, the whole world accepts him or her.” – Lao Tzu

135. "Miracles happen everyday, change your perception of what a miracle is and you'll see them all around you." – Jon Bon Jovi

136. "Owing to some peculiarity in my nervous system, I have perception of some things, which no one else has; or at least very few, if any... I can throw rays from every quarter of the universe into one vast focus." – Ada Lovelace

137. "Your perception of the world is not necessarily the same as what is actually occurring." – Peter Ralston

138. "You can go from object to object, from plant to plant, from animal to animal and regard them as symbols for the spiritual. In this way, you make your imaginative capacities fluid and release them from the sharp contours of sense perception." – Rudolf Steiner

139. "Perception is real even when it is not reality." – Edward de Bono

140. "The moment you change your perception is the moment you rewrite the chemistry of your body." – Dr. Bruce Lipton

141. "Reality is always kinder than the stories we tell about it." – Byron Katie

142. "I believe you make your day. You make your life. So much of it is all perception, and this is the form that I built for myself. I have to accept it and work within those compounds, and it's up to me." – Brad Pitt

143. "Most of us have grown up seeing the world as a place of limitation rather than as a place of inexhaustible treasures." – Bob Burg

144. "Perception precedes reality." – Andy Warhol

145. "Every beauty which is seen here by persons of perception resembles more than anything else that celestial source from which we all are come." – Michelangelo

146. "It is the function of art to renew our perception. What we are familiar with we cease to see. The writer shakes up the familiar scene, and, as if by magic, we see a new meaning in it." – Anais Nin

147. "Reality is based on perception." – Geoff Thompson

148. "The lives we live are a bit of a straight-hair vs. curly-hair thing. We often want what we don't have. In reality, it's not about better or worse; it's just perception." – Simon Sinek

149. "All our knowledge has its origins in our perceptions." – Leonardo da Vinci

150. "Perception is reality but it may not be actuality, and you have got to be able to keep the difference between that." – Bill Cowher

151. "All that we see or seem is but a dream within a dream." – Edgar Allan Poe

152. "What you see and what you hear depends a great deal on where you are standing. It also depends on what sort of person you are." – C.S. Lewis

153. "Change the way you look at things and the things you look at change." – Wayne W. Dyer

154. "To change ourselves effectively, we first had to change our perceptions." – Stephen R. Covey

155. "Always think of what is useful and not what is beautiful. Beauty will come of its own accord." – Nikolai Gogol

156. "The optimist sees the doughnut, the pessimist sees the hole." – McLandburgh Wilson

157. "One moment the world is as it is. The next, it is something entirely different. Something it has never been before." – Anne Rice

158. "Perception is reality to the one in the experience." – Danielle Bernock

159. "The truth is helpless when up against perception." – Zack W. Van

160. "Perception was easily accomplished, required little effort, and it never had to stand the test of reality." – Terry Goodkind

Closing Note

In conclusion, perception is a fundamental aspect of our lives that shapes our reality, thoughts, and behavior. This book has provided an in-depth exploration of the various ways perception impacts our lives, from personal growth to decision-making, communication, relationships, creativity, mindfulness, health, success, and the future. By understanding the power of perception and the different factors that influence it, we can take charge of our lives and improve our well-being and success.

Through the techniques and examples provided in this book, we can develop a perception awareness that empowers us to shift our mindset, improve our communication, enhance our creativity, and make better decisions. We can also use perception to improve our personal growth, relationships, and health. Finally, the book also provides insights into the future of perception and the opportunities and challenges that await us in the digital age.

In the end, the key to unlocking the power of perception lies in our ability to cultivate a growth mindset, be open to new experiences, and stay present in the moment. By doing so, we can transform our perception and unlock new possibilities for our lives. So, go ahead and unlock your reality with the power of perception!

Printed by Libri Plureos GmbH in Hamburg,
Germany